Crossing the bridge from Life to Life

REINCARNATION

WORKBOOK

Margery Phelps

author of

Finding Margaret-a case for reincarnation

Copyright 2018 by Margery Phelps.

This workbook is for the use of those interested in reincarnation, participants in my podcasts and webinars, and visitors to the website: www.FindingMargaret.com. For permission to use this material in any other setting, class, or seminar, or to purchase in bulk, please contact the copyright owner:

Margery Phelps
109 Moose Loop
Waleska, GA 30183
770-704-7662
www.Margeryphelps.com
www.CherokeeRosePublishing.com

This workbook is based on the website and book, *Finding Margaret – a case for reincarnation* and is to supplement information provided therein.

ISBN: 13: 978-0-9994622-0-1

Crossing the Bridge from Life to Life

REINCARNATION
Workbook

Dedicated to Judy and Andi

Sisters for Eternity

*"A sister is a gift to the heart,
a friend to the spirit,
a golden thread
to the meaning of life."*

Isadora James

Table of Contents

Reincarnation	1
Some Ideas to Think About	2
What is Reincarnation?`	3
Is Life a School?	5
How to use this Workbook	6
Your Early Years	9
Your Young Adult Years	15
Your Mature Life	19
Your Self-Examination	27
Putting it all together	35
Your Story	41
Examples: My Story	43
References & Links	45

Reincarnation

Finding meaning and purpose for your Life

Let's start with one simple question: **Do you believe in Eternal Life?**

If you answer "Yes" or "Maybe" this workbook is for you.

Next question: **If you believe in Eternal Life, where have you been?**

I was asked these questions by the Psychologist I consulted when I was profoundly depressed by recurring dreams of a woman I did not know. I first encountered her around age 3 or 4; she was always chasing me and saying, "Please listen; I have something important to tell you."

Although I never forgot her, age and the activities of life took away these troubling dreams until I was in my mid-forties, when she reappeared – and this time she never went away. My search for her was terrifying, to say the least – but the rewards of finding her changed my life for the better; in fact, I can say it has never been the same, and for that I am eternally grateful.

After a three-year search I found out who she was, where she lived, even the names of her children and husband.

I started listening to her, and what she said was important – very important; her simple words gave me profound insight into life. That's what I want to share with you.

I hope this workbook will give you guidance in helping you understand more about who you really are and why you are here on this amazing planet we call Earth.

Margery Phelps, Author
Finding Margaret - a case for reincarnation

Some ideas to think about

Who are we? Why are we here on this planet? How do we reconcile our spirit selves to our ego selves – our body, thoughts, habits, personality, lifestyle, etc.?

Religion and Theology

All religions and their theologians profess to know "The Truth." Because of my personal journey and discoveries, I believe every Soul must find its own truth by walking its own path. This may sound harsh or heretical (I am a devout Christian) but when you filter down through all the ego stuff -- and all the rules and regulations imposed by various cultures and religions -- ultimately our journey here is all about our own personal relationship to God.

We display our relationship to our Creator through our interactions with other Souls; if church attendance helps us have a better connection to the Divine, that's great. It does not mean that the church-goer is a better person, or more "right with God."

Questions to ponder:

What does your religion teach about reincarnation?
_____
_____

Do you agree or disagree? Why?
_____
_____

If belief in reincarnation differs from your religion, how does that make you feel?
_____
_____

What is Reincarnation?

Reincarnation – a controversial subject to be sure. A web search of "reincarnation" brings up 14 million references. Wow! How can anyone understand a subject like that?

This workbook was created to put the concept of reincarnation into basic terms that will hopefully provide useful information to help you explore the possibility of your own reincarnation and lead you into a deeper and better understanding of your own passage through life (lives). My friend, KC, says it best, "Once one is open to the concept of past lives, a whole new world of self-understanding is possible."

Understanding your past gives you a deeper, more meaningful appreciation of your current life. You will come to understand your particularly likes or dislikes: people, places, situations, talents, occupations, hobbies, family, children, elderly, races, geographic areas, politics, personal habits, living abodes…the list is as endless as life itself.

A simple explanation
- ❖ You come from a Divine and Eternal source.
- ❖ Therefore, you are Eternal.
- ❖ If you are Eternal, you have had the opportunity to visit Earth on many occasions.
- ❖ If you have visited Earth many times, you have had many lives.
- ❖ If you have had many lives, you have "reincarnated."

Why do we reincarnate?
There are as many answers to this question as there are souls walking the face of the earth. Here are a few ideas:

- ❖ We like it here:
    1. the Earth is beautiful and we want to see more of it
    2. we want to play with our Ego (temporal stuff like cars, fancy clothes, adulation)
    3. we have a desire to create on this Earth plane

- ❖ To fulfill a mission or purpose:
    1. have an experience with someone we knew in a prior life
    2. complete something we didn't do
    3. change something we did do
    4. create something to make the World better for all Souls who journey here
    5. forgive someone who hurt us
    6. love someone we hurt
    7. to have an entirely new experience
    8. to solve an on-going problem (either personal or worldly)
    9. to heal from a problem in the past

What are your ideas – why were you born in this life? To paraphrase my friend KC, many of our psychological issues, hang-ups, and blind spots can be founded in past lives. When you accept the truth of that, and focus on particular emotional issues in your life, you can tap into apparent past-originating events that explain your current issues. And you will understand that people come and go from your life, sometimes concurrently with uncovering certain past lives. KC sent me this beautiful description of what reincarnation has meant to her:

> *The comfort that the awareness of reincarnation has given me has been with me for so long, and seems so obvious, that I forget that it is a unique perspective that most people don't get to have. —The awareness of the achievements I've already had—"been there, done that," that eased the expectation on myself that I was meant to "achieve" in some grand way, this time around. —The peace that comes with realizing that if some soul desire does not get fulfilled "this time around" there is always a future life. —That we get endless chances. —That relationships that don't seem destined to be fulfilled satisfactorily in this lifetime will likely come up again, in some form, in the future. —That beloved people who have passed on will be encountered in the future, on some plane of existence, in some form or another. —That the past CAN be healed, no matter how long ago it was!*
>
> *How can people exist with the belief that this is their only lifetime? I can't even imagine feeling this way anymore. It seems an unnatural, distorted, and quite a hamstrung perspective, honestly.*

I'm sure you've heard it often: Life is a journey. By definition, that implies there is a beginning and an end. You start in one place and arrive at another and the journey is completed.

But what if you are eternal? That means there is no beginning, no end.

Is Life a School?

What if we said life is a School? If you believe that there is always something new to learn, then you would never finish. That may sound like an undaunting task to some folks, but when you think about it, with the explosion of technology, social media, and all other facets of our lives, none of us knows it all – and life is already a never-ending school. How does this relate to our Eternal Selves?

If Life is a School, doesn't it seem logical that we would progress through different levels or classes of learning? According to Brian Weiss, MD, a leading researcher and practitioner of past-life therapy, as we progress in our "spiritual schooling" (my term, not his), we must learn the lessons of immortality, anger management, health (both physical and emotional), empathy, compassion, understanding, nonviolence, relationships, security, free will and destiny, contemplation and meditation, spirituality, and the greatest lesson of all – Love.

Doesn't it seem logical then that we take the lessons and experiences of one class to the next? According to Dr. Weiss, and other experts, when we fail to learn a lesson, we repeat it in other lives until we "get it."

For this reason it is important that parents understand that their children have past lives and have their own issues to resolve. This is an entirely different scope of study being led by Gordon Keirle-Smith, the author of *Another Egg, Another Life.* (See reference on page 45.)

Perhaps then we could look at each Life time as a class room. We would be in school with other students. Some would continue into other classes with us. We would have many experiences with these other students. We would see them again and again, in one life after another. These "class mates" are our *soul mates*.

Everyone deserves a break from school now and then – remember your summer vacations from school when you were a child? When your "body" or "earth suit" is no longer useable, you take a rest in the arms of our Heavenly Father until you are ready for a new school year, and the opportunity to learn new lessons.

The soul never dies, but merely transitions back and forth from school to vacation, mortal life to soul rest. You have crossed this bridge from Eternity to Earth many times. Wouldn't you like to know where you've been?

How to use this workbook

First, before you begin ask yourself:

- What do I want to find out?
- Is there an on-going problem in my life I want to resolve?
- Am I self-disciplined to do this without harming or blaming myself or others?
- Is there a difficult relationship in my life that might be helped?
- Am I happy with my life as it is or do I feel that I need to know more?

Second, some basic guidelines:

DO NOT:
- use a psychic or website that says it will tell you about your past lives
- do not use hypnosis unless done by an expert
- do not fall into the "definition trap"
- do not get caught up in religiosity or theology
- do not believe someone who purports to know all about your past lives

DO:
- set aside some time and specific day each week to devote to your exploration
- meditate and connect to God and your higher self
- be disciplined about writing down your dreams and memories as they occur
- look for repeating themes/situations in your life (both negative and positive)
- be aware of your relationships and experiences (both good and bad)
- realize that it is YOUR class and the lessons are for YOU.

Third step – use this workbook

Record every little thought or idea that comes to you, when it comes to you. You do not have to fill in the questions in any particular order. The idea is to gather as much information as you can recall, and you will find that it skips all around – so feel free to do that in this workbook, too.

All those little details can create a big picture. Memories can come in the morning shower, or the late afternoon grocery line; while doing laundry or mowing the grass. Don't discount anything as insignificant.

When we delve into the exploration of our past lives, we must first examine our present life:
- What do we like or dislike?
- What characteristics in others do we admire or despise?
- What living environment do we prefer?
- What are we interested in?
- What activities do we prefer?
- What are our favorite subjects to study?
- What is difficult for us?
- What comes to us easily and naturally?

There are as many questions as there are souls so we can't cover all of them, but hopefully this workbook will help you uncover some key elements.

Your Early Years will get you thinking about your early childhood, since that is the time when we frequently have memories of past lives. I have given you some general ideas just to jog your memory, but you should be specific about your own experiences and memories. Please leave Page 14 blank until we get to the end; you'll need this for your *Putting it all together* section.

Your Young Adult Years explores your life and interests through high school and college. During this period we may be conflicted about our education and career goals with yearnings to do one thing, but ending up doing something different. Please leave Page 18 blank until we get to the end; you'll need this for your *Putting it all together* section.

Your Mature Life gives you questions about a variety of topics such as relationships and career. Please leave Page 26 blank until we get to the end; you'll need this for your *Putting it all together* section.

Self Examination is a series of Question & Answer Charts. This section is to help you summarize and map your own unique soul characteristics. You can qualify your feelings, either Good or Bad, for each question by putting a check-mark in the appropriate box.

Putting it all together will take you through the steps of analyzing your data and charting your Courses and at the end you will write *Your Story*.

So, let's get started!

YOUR EARLY YEARS

What is your earliest memory? Age?
Where were you? What were you wearing?
What were you doing? Who were you with?
What were you feeling?

_____

_____

_____

_____

_____

_____

Do you remember any dreams from your childhood? Did you have any dream or dreams that repeated over and over? What was happening in those dream(s)? How did you feel?

_____

_____

_____

_____

_____

Who were your parents? Did you feel especially close to one of them? Did you have any problems with either of them? Did you feel loved? Were you adopted? Who raised you? Were you close to your grandparents or some other adult?

_____

_____

_____

_____

_____

Do you have siblings? Brothers and/or sisters? How many? How much older/younger than you? Were you closer to some than to others? Why? What did you like or dislike about any of them?

_____

_____

_____

_____

_____

Where did you live? In the country or city? In a house or apartment? Who did you live with? Did you have your own room or share? Did you like where you lived? Were you happy there? Was there somewhere else you preferred to be?

_____

_____

_____

_____

What was your favorite childhood activity? Dressing up like a princess? Playing cowboy, policeman, or doctor? What was your favorite subject in Elementary School? What did you excel at? What subjects were difficult? Did you have any special interests? What did you like to read about?

_____

_____

Was there any particular object in your household that you particularly liked or disliked or feared? Where was it from?

_____

_____

_____

Who was your best childhood friend? Are you still friends? What did you enjoy doing together? What did you not like to do? Did you particularly dislike anyone? Who? Why?

_____

_____

_____

_____

Were you comfortable being a girl or a boy or did you want to be the opposite sex? Did you try to do anything about that or did you tell anyone how you felt? How did their response make you feel? Did anyone ever tell you that you looked like the opposite sex? How did you feel?

_____

_____

_____

_____

Did you have any "make believe" friends? Did you see people that no one else could see? Did you talk to them? How did they make you feel? Happy? Scared? Sad? What did you talk about? Did they tell you what to do or offer advice?

_____

_____

_____

_____

_____

What other memories do you have from your childhood? Happy? Sad? Fearful? Write down everything you can think of from your childhood that you have not already mentioned in the previous questions.

_____

_____

_____

_____

_____

Putting it all together: **Your Early Years**

YOUR YOUNG ADULT YEARS

Teenage through High School / College

Think about **your school years**. What was your favorite subject? What did you enjoy learning about? What came easily to you? What did you struggle with? Did you have a favorite teacher? Were you academically gifted in some particular subject?

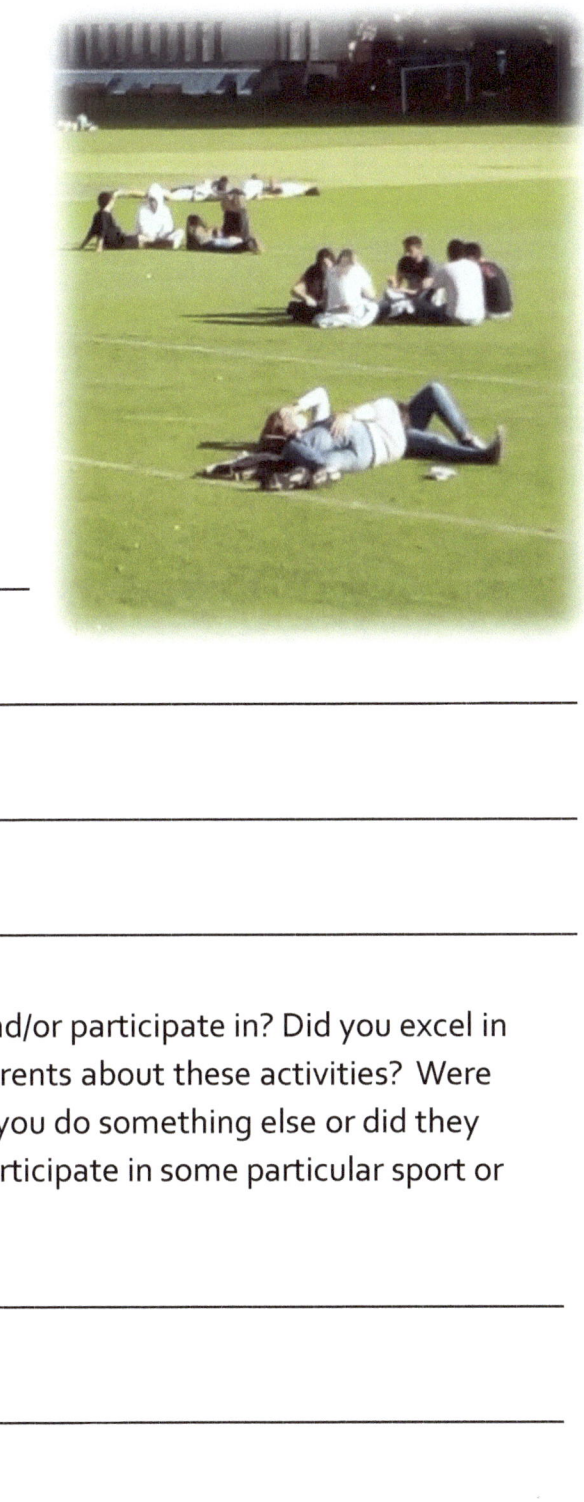

_____

_____

_____

_____

What **activities**, clubs and/or sports did you enjoy and/or participate in? Did you excel in a particular sport? Was there a conflict with your parents about these activities? Were those issues resolved? How? Did you parents want you do something else or did they support your choices? Did they demand that you participate in some particular sport or activity? How did you feel about that?

_____

_____

_____

_____

Think about your **social life**. Did you have a close friend or group of friends? Were you outgoing or quiet? Were you bullied or did you bully? What did you and your friends do together for fun? Did you attend proms or formals? Were those events important to you?

_____

_____

_____

_____

_____

_____

What about your **spiritual life**? Did you attend church/synagogue? Regularly or occasionally? Did you have friends in your religious life who were not in your social circle? Did your family say a blessing before meals? Did your parents "make" you go to church/synagogue or did you like to go? Did your parents attend also? Were religious holidays observed? Did you enjoy them? If not, why?

_____

_____

_____

_____

_____

_____

Think about the **performing arts**. Did you play a musical instrument? Did you play in a band or musical group? Did you act or participate in theatrical performances, either on stage or behind the scenes (building sets, make-up, costumes)? Do you sing? Did you have stage fright or did you always enjoy performing?

_____

_____

_____

What about **your home life** during your youth? Did you have fun or was your home life stressful? If so, why? Did you have a lot of responsibilities such as looking after younger children or sick parents? How did you feel about this?

_____

_____

_____

Did you have a **pet or other animal** *friends*? How important was your pet? What was it's name? How did you acquire that pet? Did someone give it to you or did you ask your parents if you could have it? Did it live in the house with you? How much time did you spend with your pet? Did it live a long life? How did you feel when it passed away?

_____

_____

_____

Putting it all together: **Your Young Adult Years**

YOUR MATURE LIFE

Relationships, Career, Experiences

Marriage or significant other Are you happily married? Are there problems in your relationship? If so, what? Have you been married more than one time? What was the cause of your break-up?

_____

_____

_____

Children in your life Did you want to be a parent? Do you have children? Are there other children such as nieces and nephews to whom you are particularly close? Do you have Godchildren? Do you have regular contact with children such as being a school teacher, scout leader, mentor, Sunday school teacher, etc.? How important are children to you?

_____

_____

_____

Career / Work Life What is your profession or vocation? Why did you choose that field of work? Is there something else you would prefer to do? If so, why aren't you doing that?

_____

_____

_____

Religious / Spiritual Life Do you attend church, synagogue or some other religious activity on a regular basis? Why? Are you interested in other religions? Do you have any fears related to other religions?

_____

_____

_____

Social Life Do you like to socialize? Do you enjoy parties or do you cringe at the idea of going out in the evening? Do you like to attend formal affairs or do you prefer casual gatherings? Do you like to meet new people? Is it easy or difficult for you to converse with strangers?

_____

_____

_____

Sports / Recreation Are you active in sports or recreational activities? If yes, what do you like to do? Do you participate regularly? Why did you chose this/those activities? How do you feel if you miss an event? What are your feelings about them?

_____

_____

_____

Vacations / Travels Do you travel or take vacations? Where do you like to go? Would you prefer to live at one of your travel destinations? Why? What is so appealing to you about this location?

_____

_____

_____

Civic activities / Volunteer work What civic organizations do you belong to? Why did you select that/those organizations? How active are you? How do you feel if you miss an event? Do you volunteer? Where? Why did you choose that volunteer work?

_____

_____

_____

Living Environment: Where do you live? Apartment, condo, house? Is it spacious or do you feel crowded? Do you like it here or would you prefer something else? Are you neat and clean, or do you prefer messy and cluttered? Why? Do you help to maintain the living environment or do you let /ask someone else to do it? Why?

_____

_____

_____

Clothing & Personal Appearance: Are you careful/particular about your personal appearance? Do you have healthy hygiene habits? Do you prefer expensive designer clothes, or does appearance not matter to you? Do you have tattoos and piercings? Why? Do you judge others and base relationships based on these characteristics?

_____

_____

_____

_____

Friends & Family Relationships: Think about those people with whom you have outstanding relationships as well as those that are unpleasant. Who are they? What is right and what is wrong with those relationships?

_____

_____

_____

Fears & Attractions: Do you have any fears or particularly strong attractions to wildlife, animals, objects, weather? Snakes? Spiders? Dogs? Horses? Knives? Whips? Ropes? Guns? Thunder? Lightening?

_____

_____

_____

_____

Health & Well-being Do you enjoy good health or do you have any physical challenges? What are they? How long have you had them? How do you feel about them? Are you prone to accidents? Describe your health problems/ accidents. (EX: Asthma, bad back, digestion problems, etc.)

_____

_____

_____

_____

_____

Weather conditions & Climate What is the weather where you live? Generally hot, cold, temperate? Do you enjoy living in these conditions or do you prefer something else? What type of weather would your prefer? Are you scared of threatening weather, such as hurricanes, tornadoes? Do you live near a volcano? Does it worry you?

_____

_____

_____

_____

Geographic Locations Where do you live? The beach, desert, mountains, low-country, big city, small town, rural area? Do you like it there? Why do you live there? Would you prefer to live somewhere else? Where would that be?

_____

_____

_____

_____

Objects, Collectibles & Hobbies Do you have any particular "treasures" or objects that you can't live without? What are they? Are they from a particular era or location? Did you inherit them or buy them for yourself? If you bought them, what was your thought when you made the purchase(s)? Do have collectibles? What are they and why do you collect them? Do you have a hobby? What do you do? Why are you attracted to that particular hobby/activity?

_____

_____

_____

_____

Music Do you like music? What is your favorite genre of music? Classical? Waltzes? Jazz? African? Blues? Drums? Horns? Strings? Piano? Do you know why you like it so much? How does it make you feel? Do you have any particular musical dislikes? What don't you like and why?

_____

_____

_____

_____

_____

Reading Do you like to read? What is your favorite subject? Do you prefer novels or non-fiction? Do you have a favorite author? Who? Why do you like them so much? Are there particular genres that you would never read? Why?

_____

_____

_____

_____

_____

Putting it all together: **Your Mature Life**

YOUR SELF EXAMINATION

Now that you have reviewed your life experiences, we are going to more closely examine your personal likes and dislikes (emotional **triggers**) and then see where those preferences may have impacted your life choices. When someone has a particularly strong feeling one way or the other, those feelings could be the result of a past-life experience

There is no right or wrong answer. Simply put a ✔ in the box if you have **very strong good** or **bad** feelings about each item. If you have no emotion about an item, leave it blank.

I doubt that anyone will have entries on every section; I certainly don't. Please don't feel that you are missing something if you have no triggers for that particular topic. There is a variety of topics that are generic to just about everyone; however, there is space a the bottom of each section where you can enter your own specific observations/feelings on that particular subject.

HOMES

	Good	Bad
Apartment	☐	☐
Art Deco	☐	☐
Asian / Oriental	☐	☐
Cape Cod	☐	☐
Castle	☐	☐
Contemporary	☐	☐
Cottage	☐	☐
Craftsman	☐	☐
Duplex	☐	☐
Dutch Colonial	☐	☐
Farm House	☐	☐
Federal Colonial	☐	☐
French Provincial	☐	☐
Georgian Colonial	☐	☐
Greek Revival	☐	☐
Italiante	☐	☐
Log Cabin	☐	☐
Mansion	☐	☐
Mediterranean	☐	☐
Mid-Century Modern	☐	☐
Palace	☐	☐
Prairie	☐	☐
Pueblo	☐	☐
Ranch	☐	☐
Spanish	☐	☐
Town Home	☐	☐
Trailer	☐	☐
Tudor	☐	☐
Victorian	☐	☐
Other	☐	☐

TRANSPORTATION

	Good	Bad
Airplane - Bi-plane	☐	☐
Airplane - Bomber	☐	☐
Airplane - Cargo	☐	☐
Airplane - Fighter jet	☐	☐
Airplane - Helicopter	☐	☐
Airplane - Passenger	☐	☐
Airplane - Other	☐	☐
Bicycle	☐	☐
Boat - Canoe	☐	☐
Boat - Kayak	☐	☐
Boat - Ocean freight	☐	☐
Boat - Ocean liner	☐	☐
Boat - Sailboat	☐	☐
Boat - Other	☐	☐
Bus - School	☐	☐
Bus - Public transport	☐	☐
Bus - Commuter	☐	☐
Bus - Other	☐	☐
Car - Racing	☐	☐
Car - Roadster	☐	☐
Car - Sedan	☐	☐
Car - Other	☐	☐
Hearse	☐	☐
Horse	☐	☐
Horse & buggy	☐	☐
Jeep	☐	☐
Military transport	☐	☐
Rickshaw	☐	☐
Taxi	☐	☐
Train	☐	☐
Trucks	☐	☐
Walk	☐	☐
Other	☐	☐

LOCATIONS

	Good	Bad
Back roads	☐	☐
Beaches	☐	☐
Cliffs	☐	☐
Creeks	☐	☐
Desert	☐	☐
Flat terrain	☐	☐
Forest / woods	☐	☐
Highways	☐	☐
Hilly vistas	☐	☐
Large city	☐	☐
Mountains	☐	☐
Ocean	☐	☐
Open plains	☐	☐
Rivers	☐	☐
Small town	☐	☐
Trails	☐	☐
Other	☐	☐

YOUR SELECTIONS

	Good	Bad
	☐	☐
	☐	☐
	☐	☐
	☐	☐
	☐	☐
	☐	☐

PLACES

	Good	Bad
Amphitheater	☐	☐
Arena (sports)	☐	☐
Business office	☐	☐
Castle	☐	☐
Church	☐	☐
Dock / pier / port	☐	☐
Feed / livestock store	☐	☐
Grocery store	☐	☐
Hardware store	☐	☐
Hospital	☐	☐
Library	☐	☐
Manufacturing plant	☐	☐
Medical/Dental office	☐	☐
Mosque	☐	☐
Old folks home	☐	☐
Pharmacy	☐	☐
Rail yard	☐	☐
Rehab center	☐	☐
Restaurants	☐	☐
School	☐	☐
Ship yard	☐	☐
Shopping mall	☐	☐
Small store	☐	☐
Synagogue	☐	☐
Theatre	☐	☐
Warehouse	☐	☐
Playground	☐	☐
Other	☐	☐

EVENTS

	Good	Bad
Anniversaries	☐	☐
Baptisms	☐	☐
Birthdays	☐	☐
Christmas	☐	☐
Easter	☐	☐
Fourth of July	☐	☐
Funerals	☐	☐
Hanukkah	☐	☐
Holy Days	☐	☐
Homecoming	☐	☐
Labor Day	☐	☐
Memorial Day	☐	☐
Passover	☐	☐
Proms	☐	☐
Thanksgiving	☐	☐
Valentines	☐	☐
Veteran's Day	☐	☐
Weddings	☐	☐
Other	☐	☐

NAMES of PEOPLE

	Good	Bad
	☐	☐
	☐	☐
	☐	☐
	☐	☐
	☐	☐
	☐	☐

COLORS

	Good	Bad
Black	☐	☐
Blue	☐	☐
Brown	☐	☐
Brunette	☐	☐
Charcoal	☐	☐
Cinnamon	☐	☐
Crimson	☐	☐
Ebony	☐	☐
Fuchsia	☐	☐
Gold	☐	☐
Green	☐	☐
Grey	☐	☐
Lavender	☐	☐
Lime	☐	☐
Mauve	☐	☐
Navy	☐	☐
Olive	☐	☐
Orange	☐	☐
Pink	☐	☐
Purple	☐	☐
Red	☐	☐
Ruby	☐	☐
Tan	☐	☐
Tangerine	☐	☐
Teal	☐	☐
Violet	☐	☐
White	☐	☐
Yellow	☐	☐
Other	☐	☐

We have more questions to ask about PEOPLE; you may have additional characteristics to qualify, so you will see a section at the bottom of the page to fill in as you like. Remember, we are talking about your feelings and strong emotions here; there is no right or wrong answer.

RACE:	Good	Bad
African-American/Black	☐	☐
Alaskan Native	☐	☐
American Indian	☐	☐
Caucasian/White	☐	☐
Hispanic/Latino	☐	☐
Pacific Islander	☐	☐

SKIN COLOR / COMPLEXION	Good	Bad
Dark	☐	☐
Freckles	☐	☐
Light	☐	☐
Olive	☐	☐
Pale	☐	☐
Tan	☐	☐

HAIR	Good	Bad
Bald	☐	☐
Black	☐	☐
Blond	☐	☐
Brown	☐	☐
Curly	☐	☐
Frizzy	☐	☐
Grey	☐	☐
Long	☐	☐
Receding	☐	☐
Red	☐	☐
Short	☐	☐
Straight	☐	☐
White	☐	☐
Other	☐	☐

EYES	Good	Bad
Amber	☐	☐
Blue	☐	☐
Brown	☐	☐
Green	☐	☐
Grey	☐	☐
Hazel	☐	☐

YOUR SELECTIONS	Good	Bad
	☐	☐
	☐	☐
	☐	☐
	☐	☐
	☐	☐
	☐	☐

BODY/BUILD

	Good	Bad
Buff	☐	☐
Overweight	☐	☐
Petite	☐	☐
Plump	☐	☐
Short	☐	☐
Skinny	☐	☐
Slim	☐	☐
Stocky	☐	☐
Tall	☐	☐
Trim	☐	☐
Well-built	☐	☐
Other	☐	☐

SHOES

	Good	Bad
Boots	☐	☐
Dress shoes	☐	☐
High heels	☐	☐
Loafers	☐	☐
Moccasins	☐	☐
Sandals	☐	☐
Slippers	☐	☐
Tennis shoes	☐	☐
Other	☐	☐

CLOTHING

	Good	Bad
Ball gowns	☐	☐
Coats, Jackets, waistcoats	☐	☐
Formal wear	☐	☐
Head-dresses / crowns / hats / turbans / veils / wigs	☐	☐
Leathers / Animal skins	☐	☐
Long dresses	☐	☐
Military uniforms	☐	☐
Overalls / dungarees	☐	☐
Sari	☐	☐
Shawl / scarf	☐	☐
Toga / tunic	☐	☐
Suits	☐	☐
Sweaters / pullovers	☐	☐
Trousers / pants / breeches	☐	☐
Suspenders / belts	☐	☐
Tuxedos	☐	☐
Work Uniforms	☐	☐
Other	☐	☐

OTHER ITEMS

	Good	Bad
	☐	☐
	☐	☐
	☐	☐
	☐	☐
	☐	☐

PHYSICAL CHALLENGES	Good	Bad
Ankles	☐	☐
Arms	☐	☐
Bladder	☐	☐
Brain	☐	☐
Ears / Hearing	☐	☐
Elbows	☐	☐
Eyes / Vision Seeing	☐	☐
Feet	☐	☐
Fingers	☐	☐
Hair	☐	☐
Hands	☐	☐
Head	☐	☐
Heart	☐	☐
Hips	☐	☐
Intestinal	☐	☐
Kidneys	☐	☐
Knees	☐	☐
Legs	☐	☐
Low back	☐	☐
Lungs	☐	☐
Mouth	☐	☐
Neck	☐	☐
Nerves	☐	☐
Nose / smell	☐	☐
Skin / complexion	☐	☐
Spine	☐	☐
Stomach	☐	☐
Tongue	☐	☐
Voice / speaking	☐	☐
Wrists	☐	☐
Other	☐	☐

APTITUDES	Good	Bad
Acting	☐	☐
Arithmetic / math	☐	☐
Artistic	☐	☐
Attention to details	☐	☐
Chemistry	☐	☐
Communications	☐	☐
Concentration	☐	☐
Counseling	☐	☐
Creativity	☐	☐
Designing	☐	☐
Engineering (any field)	☐	☐
Focus	☐	☐
Languages	☐	☐
Learning	☐	☐
Librarian	☐	☐
Literature	☐	☐
Medical (any field)	☐	☐
Music	☐	☐
Nursing	☐	☐
Physics	☐	☐
Reading	☐	☐
Research	☐	☐
Self-starter	☐	☐
Teaching	☐	☐
Technology	☐	☐
Writing	☐	☐
Others	☐	☐
	☐	☐
	☐	☐
	☐	☐

EMOTIONS

	Good	Bad
Abandoned	☐	☐
Angry	☐	☐
Appreciative	☐	☐
Boastful	☐	☐
Combative	☐	☐
Confident	☐	☐
Envious	☐	☐
Fearful	☐	☐
Friendly	☐	☐
Frustrated easily	☐	☐
Gratitude	☐	☐
Guilt / Shame	☐	☐
Joyful	☐	☐
Judgmental	☐	☐
Lonely / isolated	☐	☐
Loved	☐	☐
Loyal	☐	☐
Modest	☐	☐
Optimistic	☐	☐
Pessimistic	☐	☐
Rational	☐	☐
Sad / depressed / anxious	☐	☐
Shy	☐	☐
Socializing	☐	☐
Stable relationships	☐	☐
Trusting	☐	☐
Others	☐	☐
	☐	☐
	☐	☐

SPIRITUAL

	Good	Bad
Compassionate	☐	☐
Considerate	☐	☐
Contemplative	☐	☐
Devout	☐	☐
Forgiving	☐	☐
Honest	☐	☐
Hopeful	☐	☐
Humble	☐	☐
Introspective	☐	☐
Intuitive	☐	☐
Kind	☐	☐
Patient	☐	☐
Peaceful	☐	☐
Persevering	☐	☐
Prayerful	☐	☐
Resilient	☐	☐
Selfless	☐	☐
Tolerant	☐	☐
Others	☐	☐
	☐	☐
	☐	☐
	☐	☐

Putting it all together

There are some memories of past lives that impact us, even though we are unaware that those feelings are generated by a past-life, and hopefully the previous exercises have jogged your memory and brought some of these to your attention.

To illustrate how this works, here's an example from my own life. To protect the identities of the family and town involved, I'll use "E-family" and "T-town" to describe them.

When I was about 12 years old, a new family moved into our neighborhood, and since my twin sister and I were the local babysitters, they asked us to take care of their two little girls. As soon as we met the E-family I felt a connection to them that my 12-year old mind could not describe. Every time they called us, I told my sister that I HAD to go take care of those little girls. I adored their Mom and Dad, but mostly, I just LOVED their family name. I would say it over and over and over again.

Another name I loved was "Margaret." My older brother was dating a girl at our church with that name, and I thought it was the most beautiful sound I had ever heard. I wanted to know all about her. I was almost obsessed with her name.

Even though I was busy with the standard affairs of life, marriage, career, and raising two children, I never forgot Margaret and the E-family names. Then, in 1978, when I was 34 years old, I went to work for an attorney, who told me he was from T-town. I almost went off the deep end asking him questions about that small Georgia town that few people knew of. Was it a nice place? What was the school like? Did they have a church? On and on I asked. I was sure he must think me crazy to be so preoccupied with his home town.

Although I had heard of reincarnation, it was not part of my belief system. I thought the idea sounded nice – that we are eternal and our Souls never die, and can therefore come and go from the Earth.

Fast forward to 1987. A little grey-haired woman I had dreamed about as a very young child suddenly reappeared in my dreams, and I even had visions of her. One thing led to another, and I ultimately worked with a parapsychologist to unravel the feelings and emotions I was having related to these strange happenings about someone I did not know.

Well, lo and behold. In a trance session, I described this little lady, where she lived, and gave my psychologist details of her family.

Her name was Margaret E-family and she lived in T-town.

I had NEVER been to T-town. Then, a year later, my college-student daughter started dating a fellow student, and guess where he was from? Yep! T-town. When I visited there, I knew exactly where Margaret's grave was.

I hope this true story will illustrate for you how our past-life memories and feelings can and do manifest themselves in our current lives. My friend, Louisa Hickman, took this picture of me at Margaret's grave in 1995 in T-town. My life has never been the same, and I can honestly say that I have no fear of "dying" because I know for certain that Life Is Eternal. (I photo-shopped the tombstone to eliminate her name to protect the privacy of her family.)

I hope this story will show you how things or situations we think are insignificant, or not important, can actually have a huge impact on our lives once we know the true source. So, where have you been in your past? What did you do? Who did you love? Were you sick or injured? What has all that got to do with your current life?

To help you on your exploration into your past lives, I've given you some examples from my own discoveries on page 43, *My Story*, since mine have been documented, and I don't like to use purely anecdotal illustrations from sources that can't be verified.

1. Review *Your Early Years*, pages 9 - 13, and write your summary on page 14.

2. Review *Your Young Adult Years*, pages 15 - 17, and write your summary on page 18.

3. Review *Your Mature Life*, pages 19 - 25, and write your summary on page 26.

4. Review *Your Self Examination*, pages 27 - 34. Starting on page 38 you can summarize your findings from the *Self Examination* charts. Don't worry if there are a lot of blanks; some charts may have no entry at all. That's okay. These are just ideas to jog your memories.

5. The last few pages, *Your Story*, starting on page 41, are for you to record your overall feelings and memories, what your challenges have been in this life, and what you have learned or need to learn.

Putting it all together: **Your Self Examination**

Here are all the categories on the previous charts. Review those charts and write a brief summary here for each chart.

HOMES:
_____
_____

TRANSPORTATIONS:
_____
_____

LOCATIONS:
_____
_____

PLACES:
_____
_____

YOUR SELECTIONS:
_____
_____

EVENTS:
_____
_____

COLORS:
_____
_____

NAMES OF PEOPLE:
_____
_____

RACE:
_____
_____

HAIR:
_____
_____

SKIN COLOR / COMPLEXION:
_____
_____

EYES:
_____
_____

YOUR SELECTIONS:
_____
_____

BODY / BUILD:

CLOTHING:

SHOES:

OTHER ITEMS:

PHYSICAL CHALLENGES:

APTITUDES:

ANY ITEMS NOT OTHERWISE SELECTED:

Your Story

Your story will help you answer questions, resolve problems. After noticing what is going on in your life and making entries in your workbook, you will begin to see repetitive patterns; these are the keys to unlocking your past lives.

In writing *Your Story*, think about the spiritual lessons you have learned, or want to learn, so that your future lives will not be encumbered with unresolved issues. (Refer to page 5 for the list of Spiritual Schooling Lessons.)

_____

_____

_____

_____

_____

_____

_____

_____

_____

_____

_____

_____

Your Story (continued)

My Story – past-life connections to the present

Here are some examples of my memories, likes, dislikes, created by past-life situations:

- I have always hated cold water; as a child the first plunge into the swimming pool caused me an inordinate amount of stress and I feared it would kill me. When I did a past life regression with my psychologist (in my forties), my soul was a very small girl who fell into a freezing cold, fast-moving river. She died from her exposure to the cold water.

- Since age 4, I have been physically challenged with lung problems; this situation was exacerbated at age 53 when I was poisoned by toxic fumes in an upscale (Gables Residential, Inc.) apartment. In a past-life regression, my soul was incarnated in a small child who was killed by suffocating fumes during the eruption of Mt. Vesuvius in Pompeii in 79 A.D. She died in her mother's arms.

- My twin sister and I loved to go to the feed store with our grandmother because she let us pick out the feed bags, which were made of muslin cotton fabric with a variety of patterns that she would turn into sundresses and hats for us. In a past-life regression, my soul was a 9-10 year old girl who lived on the plains near Goshen, Wyoming, and she wore muslin clothes and hat.

- I loved going to my grandparents small farm, where we planted vegetables, took care of the chickens and collected eggs daily, helped with the formal rose garden, and ate meals cooked on a wood stove. (My grandmother had a large kitchen with two stoves, electric and wood. We always preferred food cooked on the wood stove.) When I found Margaret, I learned that her husband had been a farmer.

- From the earliest age I loved babies and small children, and started baby sitting before I was 12, because I was so good with the little folks. Margaret had nine children in 18 years, and most of them died in infancy or early childhood. This also accounts for my passion for children's health and nutrition, and my 20-year work in that field.

- Childhood play with friends always involved building a fort or cabin. This hearkens back to the Goshen, Wyoming days as a young child in the 1850's.

- I read every book in the school library related to the Old West, Pony Express, and any other topic of that era. Again, this obsession with that period of time goes back two life-times, to Wyoming.

- My trip to Ireland in 2016 was eye-opening. In Dublin, I seemed to know where everything was located, and people actually stopped me on the street to ask me for directions. I don't know what past-life my soul enjoyed in this amazing country, but it is something I do want to explore.

My Story, continued

Other memories of past-lives that I have experienced:

- Ball gowns and trunks – Vienna in the 1760's
- Button and laced boots – Wyoming, 1850's
- Tunics or chitons – Ancient Greece
- Sailing ships – England in 1760's
- Dark green velvet – Boston in 1750's

My Story – lessons learned

Here are some examples of lessons I've learned in this life as a result of *seeing the big picture* of my soul's schooling. Applying past-life lessons to our current life gives us peace and understanding and moves us forward into the next life without all the baggage of unresolved conflicts.

- I was generally afraid of my mom, and for that reason learned to depend on my "special feelings" (ESP) to navigate my relationship with her. As a 17-year old, this ESP saved her life when 123 other people were killed in Orly, France in 1962. It took me many years to realize this fear was instrumental in my learning some of my great lessons in this lifetime, and it was actually my training ground to hone skills of empathy and perception that I have used all my life. For that reason, I now say that I had a truly Great Mom, because she prepared me for the life I was to live.

- My husband's mother was emotionally, physically and financially cruel to me. I have never found her in a past-life; however, I know in my heart that I have to forgive her for what she did so that I won't carry her animosity toward me into another life that might cause me to seek out revenge on her.

- I was married for almost 25 years, and have been single for 28 years now. I never remarried, preferring to make a happy life for myself. Margaret's husband pre-deceased her by almost 30 years, so she was alone many years, too. In the 5th to 4th century BC, my soul was a seer in Greece, who abandoned her role to protect her people when she dallied around with a man. She fled to Egypt, where she lived out her life alone, without a mate. When people ask me why I'm not lonely because I'm not married, I tell them that it is my soul's choice and I am never lonely. I've learned that when you know without a doubt that you are always a part of the One, that you are never alone.

References & Links

Brian L. Weiss, MD

Website: http://www.brianweiss.com/
Books: *Many Lives, Many Masters*
Same Soul, Many Bodies
Through Time into Healing
Only Love is Real

Carol Bowman

Websites: https://www.carolbowman.com/
https://www.carolbowman.com/reincarnation-forum
Books: *Children's Past Lives*
Return from Heaven

Gordon Keirle-Smith

Websites: http://www.genesis-antarctica.com/gordon-keirle-smith/
http://genesis-antarctica.com/aeal/
Books: *Another Egg, Another Life* (Children's Activity Book and Grown-Ups Book)
Genesis Antarctica

Ian Stevenson, MD

Websites: https://med.virginia.edu/perceptual-studies/who-we-are/dr-ian-stevenson/
https://www.near-death.com/reincarnation/research/ian-stevenson.html
Books: *Children Who Remember Previous Lives*
Where Reincarnation and Biology Intersect

Richard Martini

Website: http://www.richmartini.com/
Book: *Flipside: A Journey to the Afterlife*

Quantum Healing Hypnosis Technique by Dolores Cannon

Website: https://www.qhhtofficial.com/

Books: *Five Lives Remembered*
Legacy from the Stars
Keepers of the Garden
Jesus and the Essenes
Convoluted Universe

The Newton Institute (Michael Newton, PhD)

Website: https://www.newtoninstitute.org/

Books: *Journey of Souls*
Destiny of Souls
Memories of the Afterlife

The Institute for the Integration of Science, Intuition and Spirit

Website: https://reincarnationresearch.com/

Reincarnation: A Journey through Cultures and Religions
A Path to Peace
Children's Past Lives

Books by Walter Semkiw, MD, MPH-Reincarnation Research:

Return of the Revolutionaries: The Case for Reincarnation and Soul Groups Reunited
Born Again

SUGGESTED READING

Across Time and Death – A Mother's Search for her Past-Life Children
by Jenny Cockell

To Heaven and Back: A Doctor's Extraordinary Account of Her Death, Heaven, Angels, and Life Again: A True Story
by Mary C. Neal, MD

Proof of Heaven: A Neurosurgeon's Journey into the Afterlife
by Eben Alexander, MD

Return to Life: Extraordinary Cases of Children Who Remember Past Lives
By Jim Tucker, MD

Reincarnation – The Missing Link in Christianity
by Elizabeth Clare Prophet and Erin L. Prophet

www.ingramcontent.com/pod-product-compliance
Lightning Source LLC
Chambersburg PA
CBHW041534040426
42446CB00002B/80